SIMPLE ARRANGEMENTS FOR STUDENT

Shake It Off, All About That Bass & More Hot Singles

Contents

ISBN 978-1-4950-1298-3

HAL•LEONARD®
CORPORATION

7777 W. BLUEMOUND RD. P.O. BOX 13819 MILWAUKEE, WI 53213

Visit Hal Leonard Online at
www.halleonard.com

ALL ABOUT THAT BASS

Words and Music by KEVIN KADISH
and MEGHAN TRAINOR

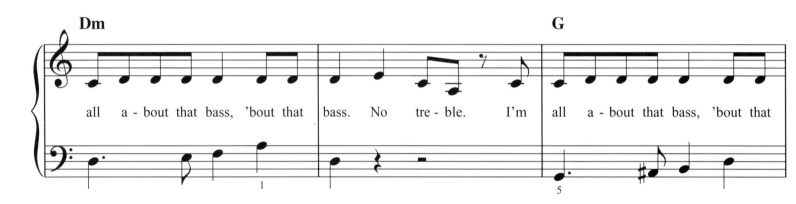

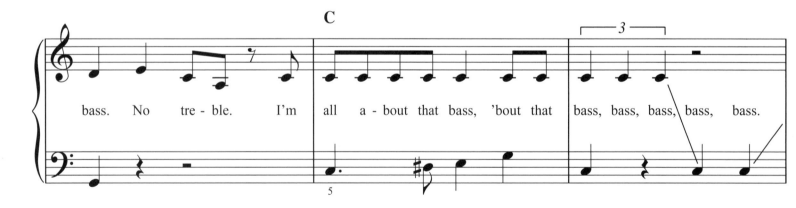

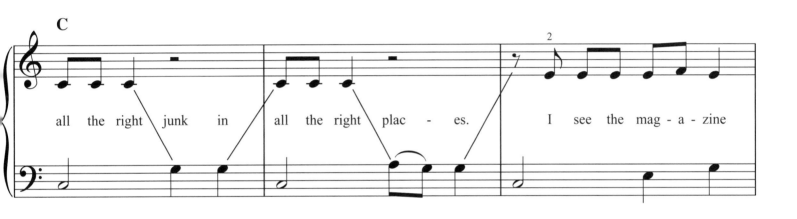

4

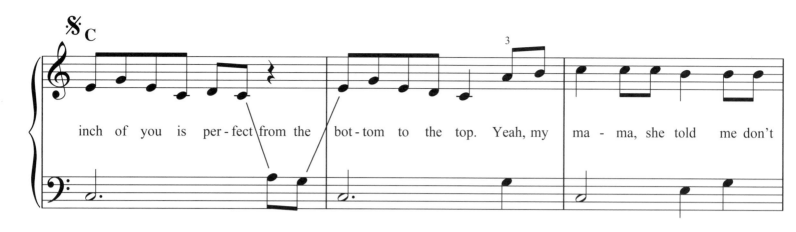

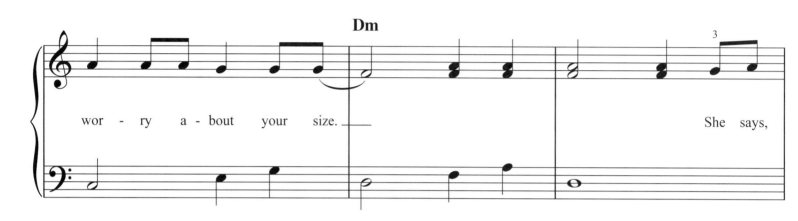

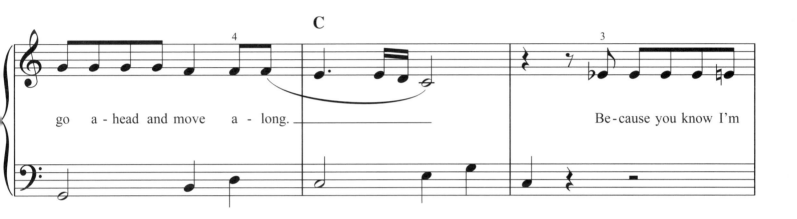

6

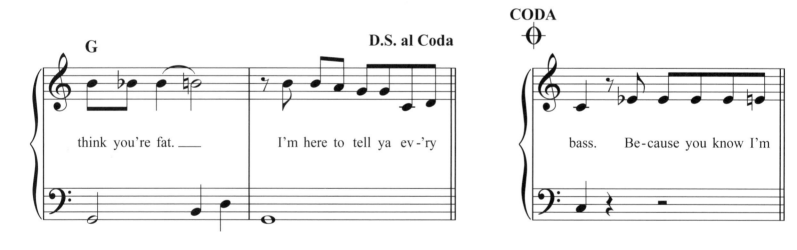

SHAKE IT OFF

Words and Music by TAYLOR SWIFT,
MAX MARTIN and SHELLBACK

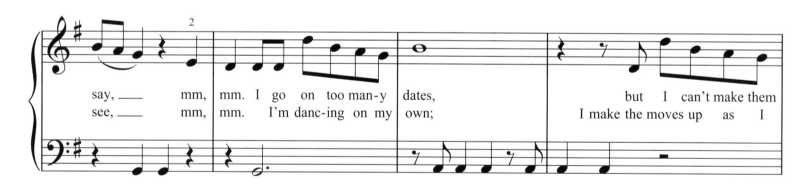

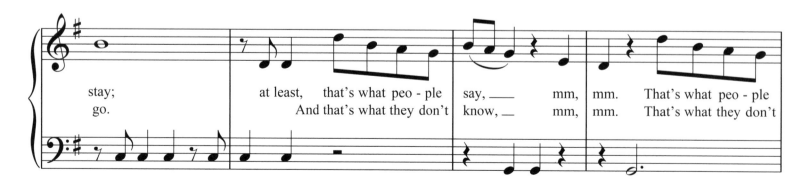

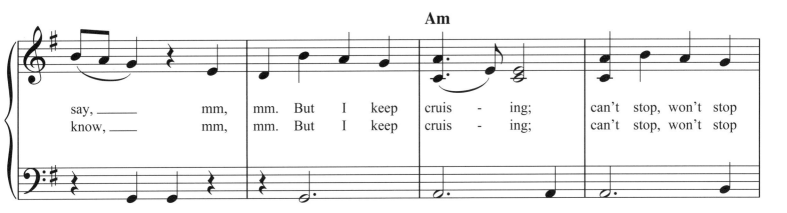

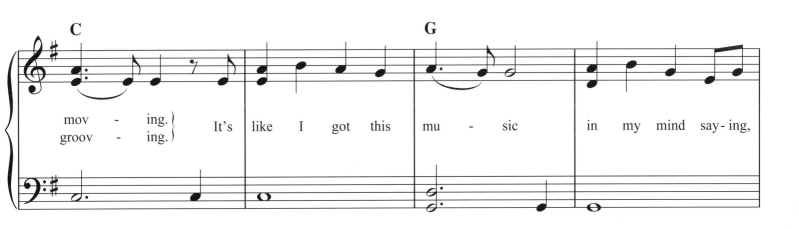

shake, shake, shake; — I shake it off, I shake it off. (Ooh, — ooh!) Heart-

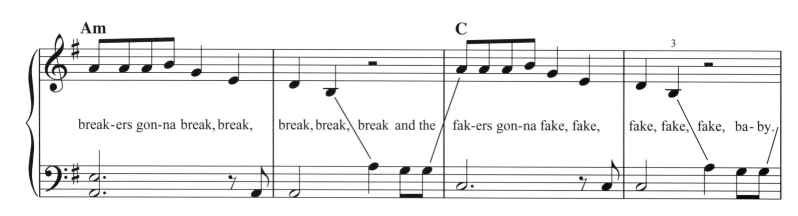

break-ers gon-na break, break, break, break, break and the fak-ers gon-na fake, fake, fake, fake, fake, ba- by.

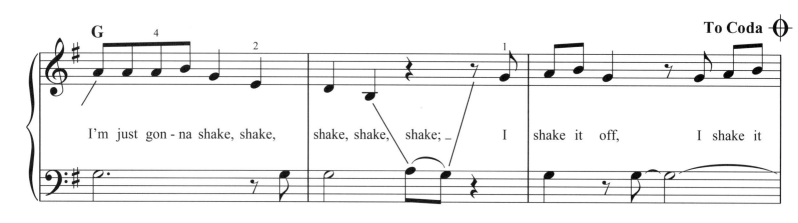

I'm just gon - na shake, shake, shake, shake, shake; — I shake it off, I shake it

off. I nev-er miss a off. (Ooh, — ooh!) I shake it off, I shake it off. I, I, I

C   G

shake it off,   I shake it off. I, I, I   shake it off,   I shake it off. I, I, I

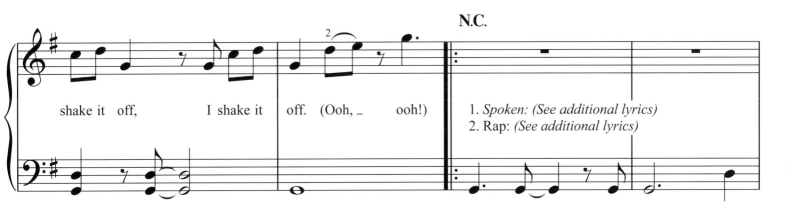

N.C.

shake it off,   I shake it off. (Ooh, _ ooh!)   1. *Spoken: (See additional lyrics)*

2. Rap: *(See additional lyrics)*

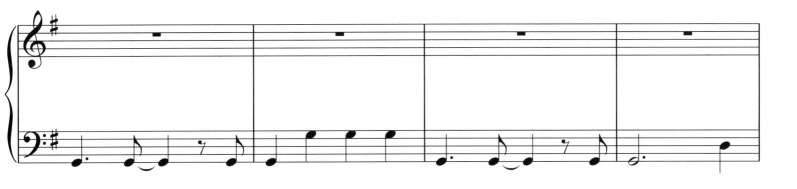

D.S. al Coda

Rap ends   Yeah, _ oh. _____ 'Cause the

12

Additional Lyrics

Spoken: Hey, hey, hey! Just think: While you've been getting
Down and out about the liars and the dirty, dirty
Cheats of the world, you could've been getting down to
This. Sick. Beat!

Rap: My ex-man brought his new girlfriend.
She's like, "Oh, my god!" But I'm just gonna shake.
And to the fella over there with the hella good hair,
Won't you come on over, baby? We can shake, shake, shake.

SOMETHING IN THE WATER

Words and Music by CHRIS DESTEFANO,
CARRIE UNDERWOOD and BRETT JAMES

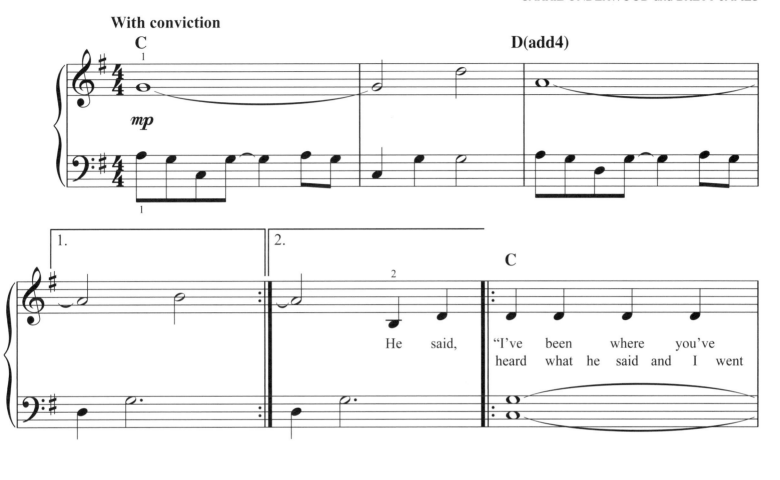

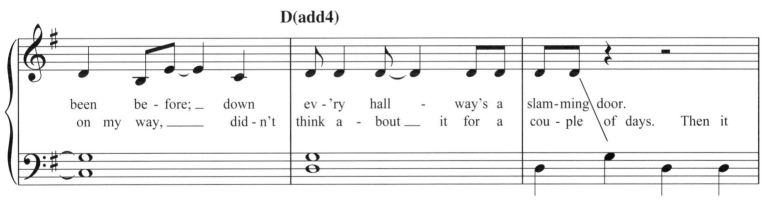

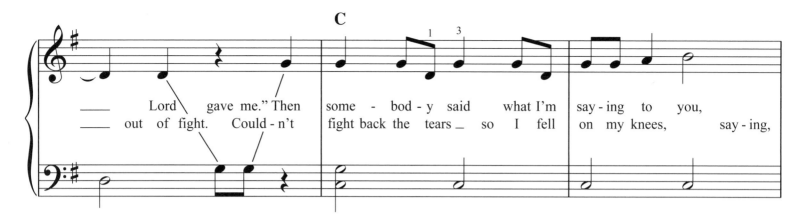

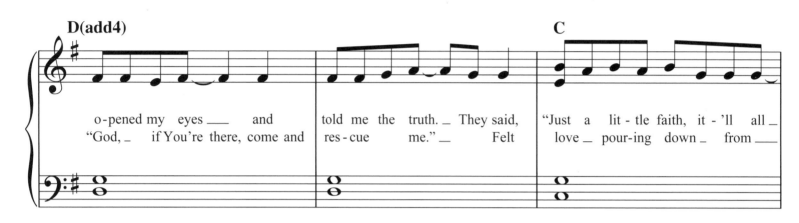

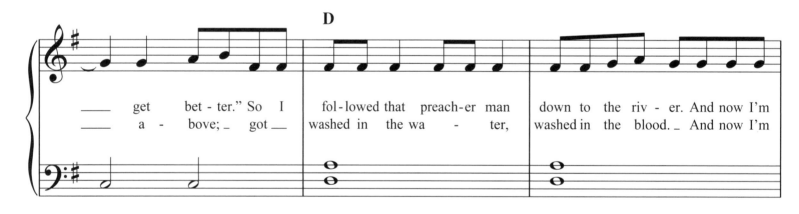

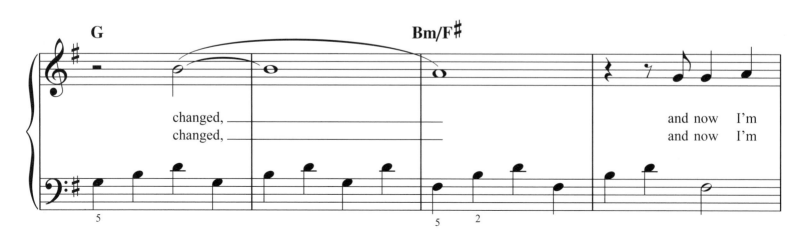

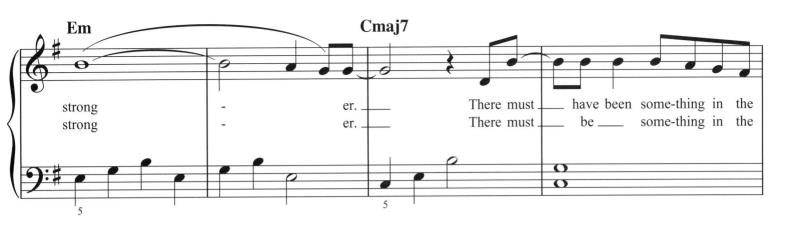

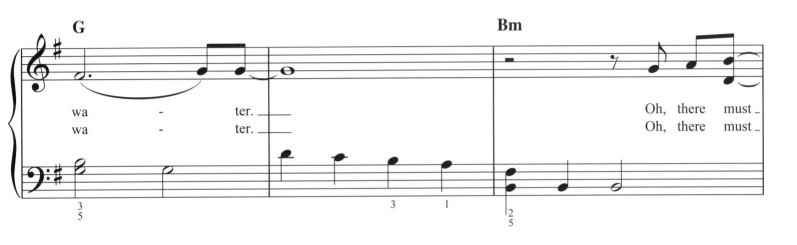

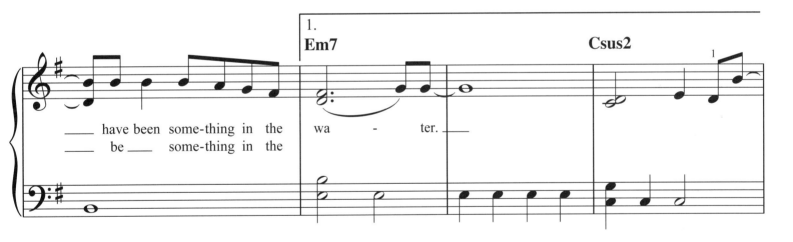

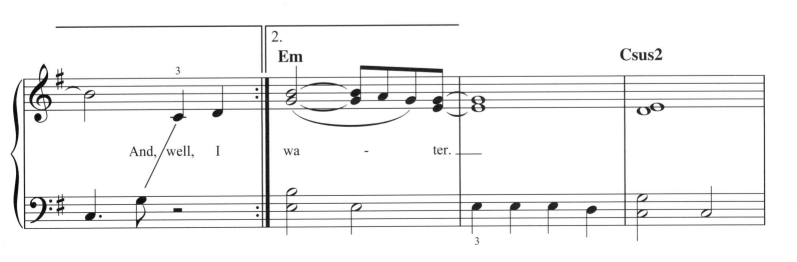

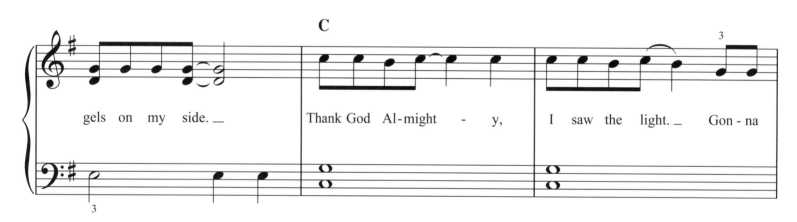

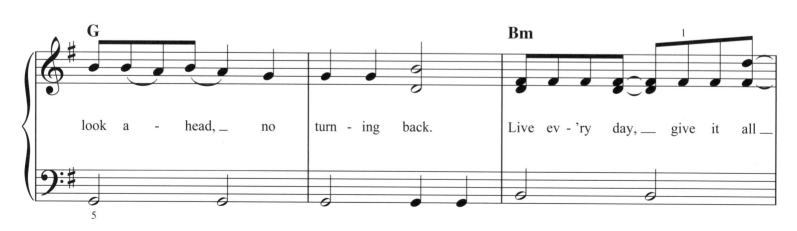

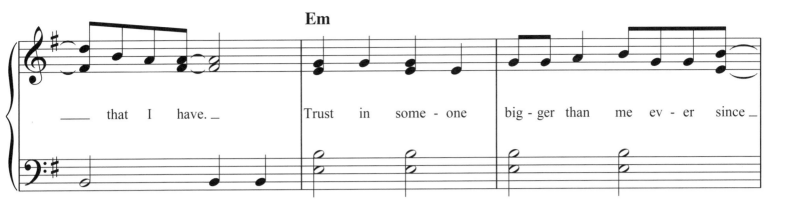

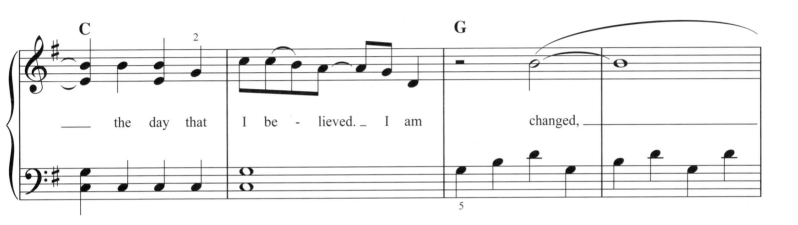

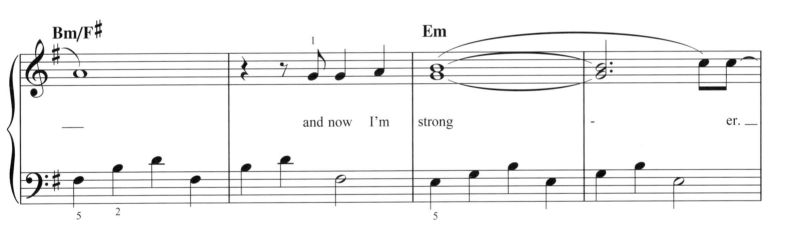

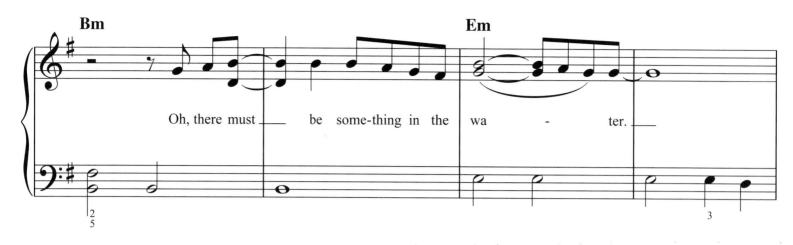

Oh, there must ___ be some-thing in the wa - ter. ___

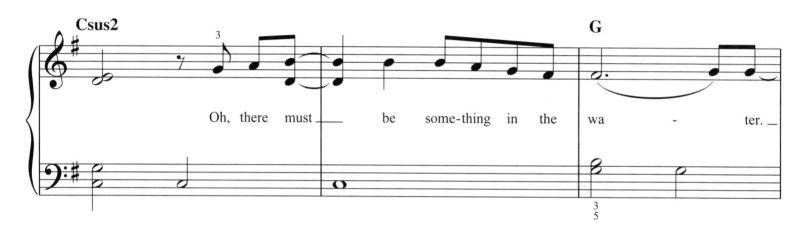

Oh, there must ___ be some-thing in the wa - ter. ___

Oh, there must ___ be some-thing in the

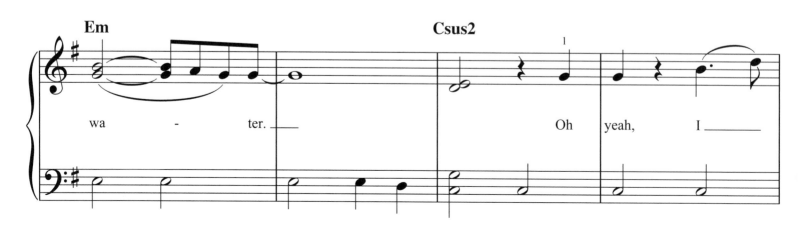

wa - ter. ___ Oh yeah, I ___

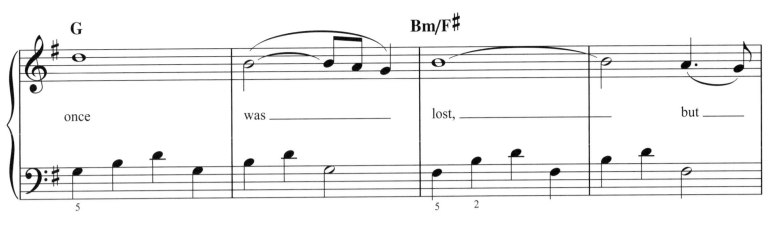

once | was _____ | lost, _____ | but _____

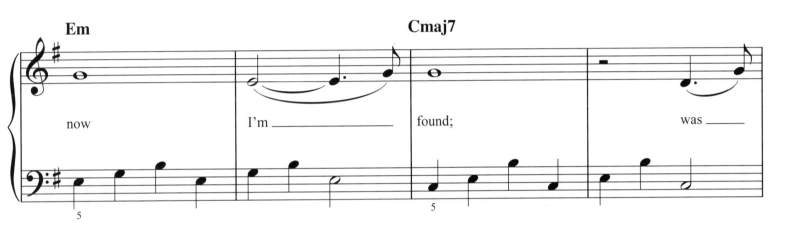

now | I'm _____ | found; | was _____

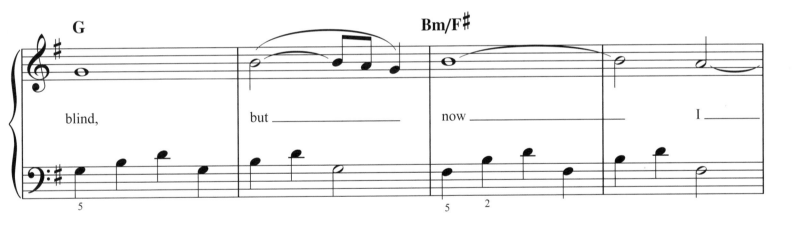

blind, | but _____ | now _____ | I _____

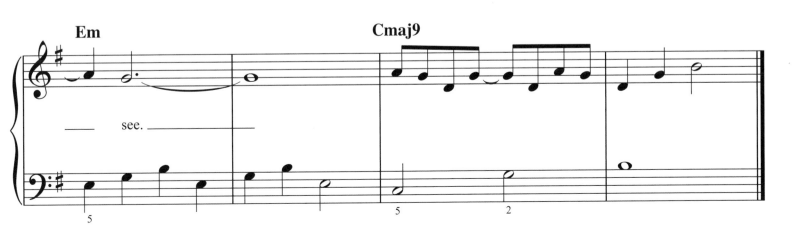

_____ see. _____

A SKY FULL OF STARS

Words and Music by GUY BERRYMAN,
JON BUCKLAND, WILL CHAMPION,
CHRIS MARTIN and TIM BERGLING

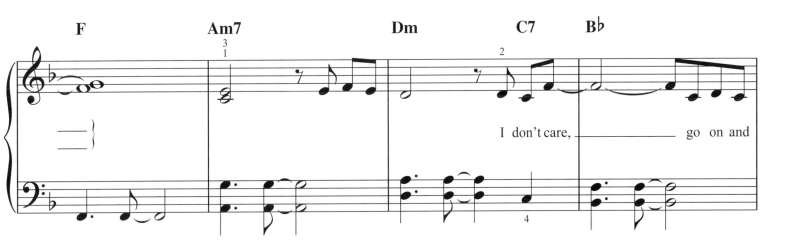

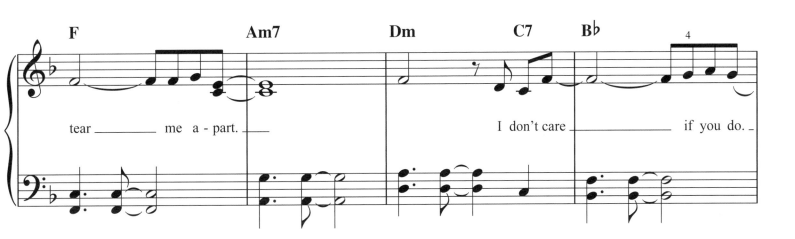

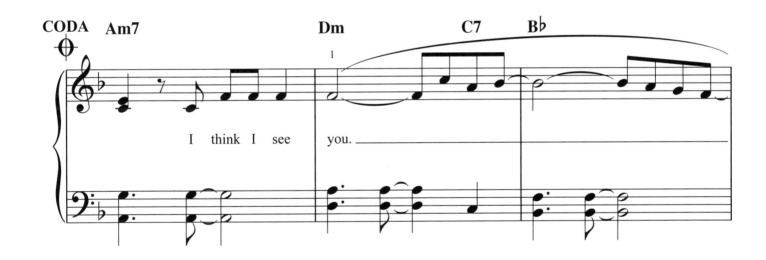

I think I see you.

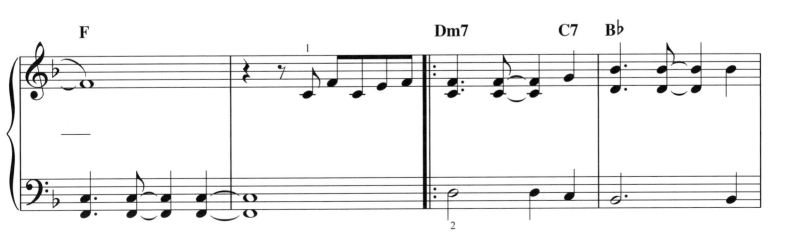

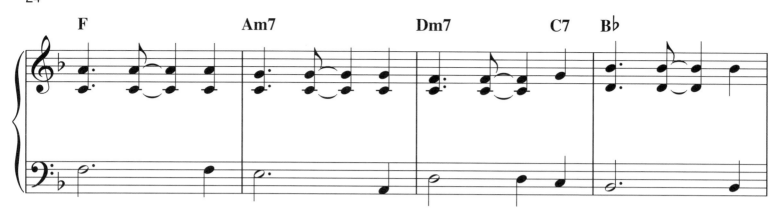

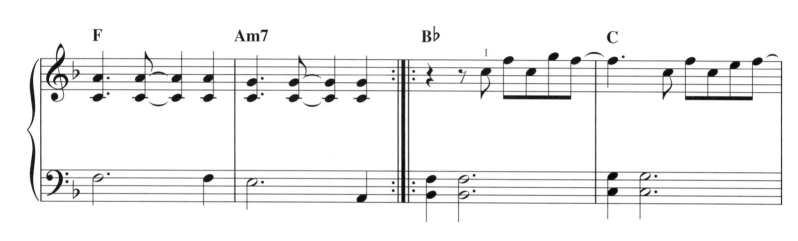

'Cause you're a sky, _

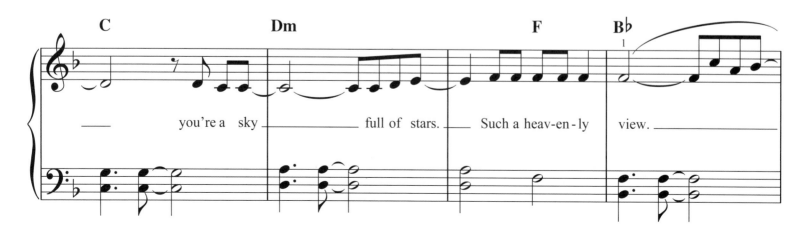

_ you're a sky _ full of stars. _ Such a heav-en-ly view. _

You're such a heav-en-ly view.

TAKE ME TO CHURCH

Words and Music by
ANDREW HOZIER-BYRNE

Piano Ballad

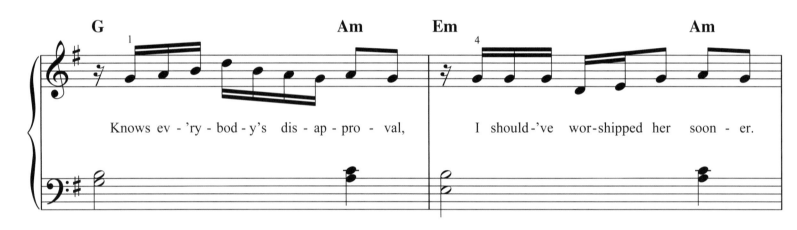

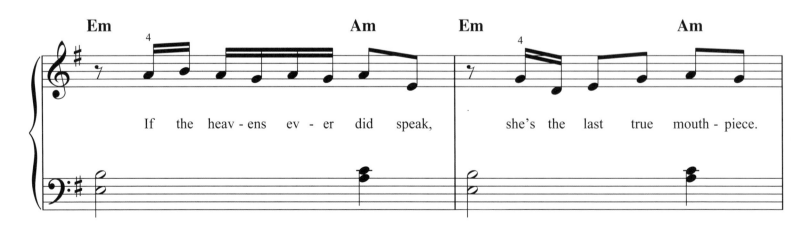

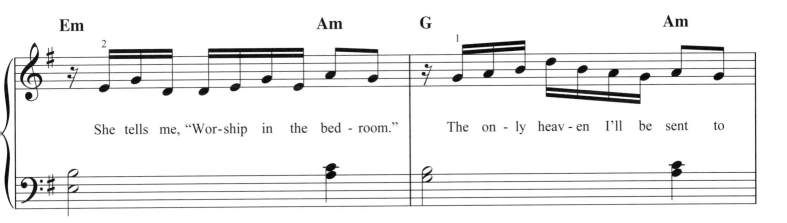

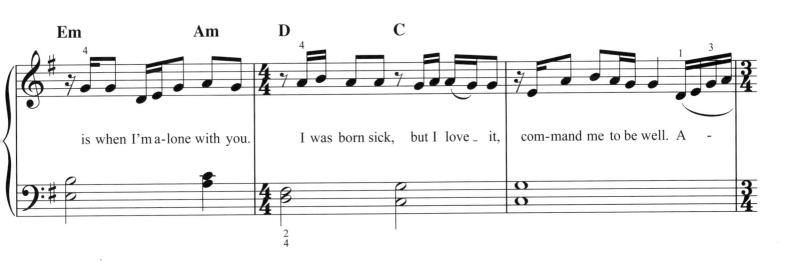

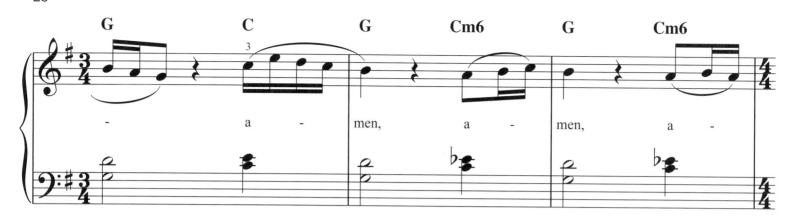

- a - men, a - men, a -

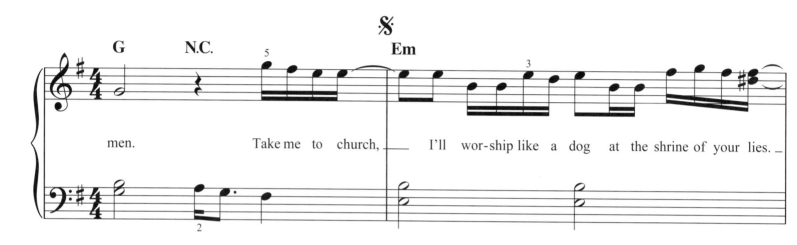

men. Take me to church, ___ I'll wor-ship like a dog at the shrine of your lies. _

___ I'll tell you my sins ___ and you can sharp-en your knife. ___ Of-fer me ___ that death-less death and, good

God, let me give you my life. Take me to church, ___ I'll wor-ship like a dog at the shrine of your lies. _

I'll tell you my sins __ and you can sharp-en your knife. __ Of-fer me __ that death-less death and, good

God, let me give you my life. If I'm a pa-gan of the good times,

my lov-er's the sun-light. To keep the god-dess on my side, she de-mands a sac-ri-fice.

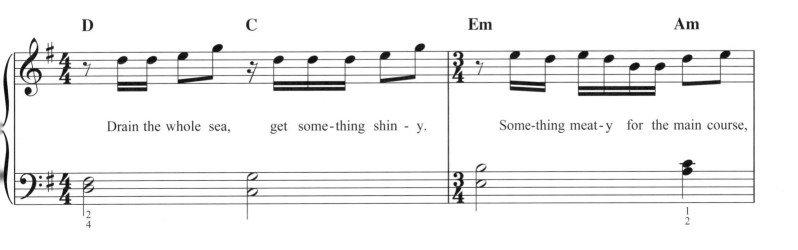

Drain the whole sea, get some-thing shin-y. Some-thing meat-y for the main course,

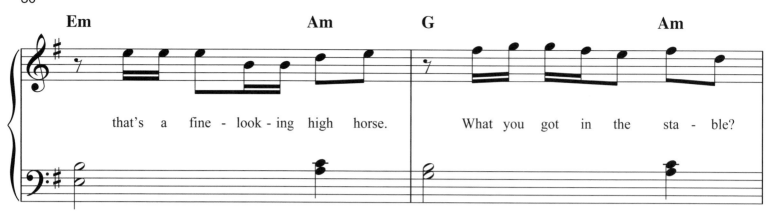

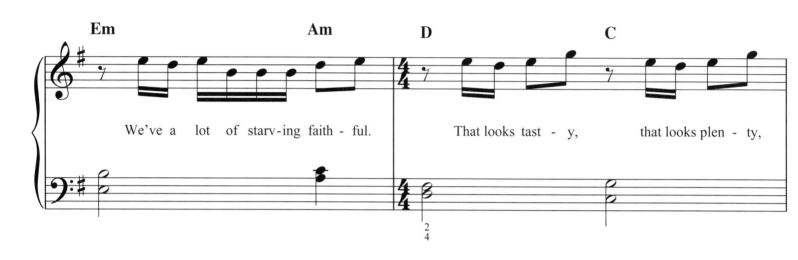

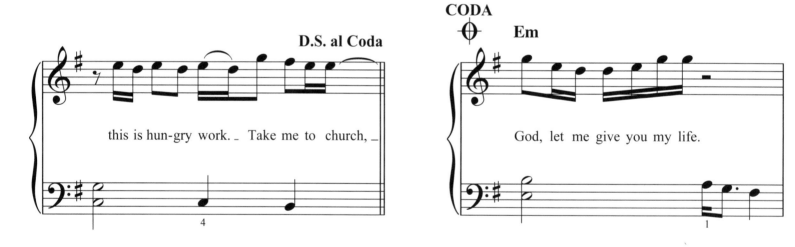

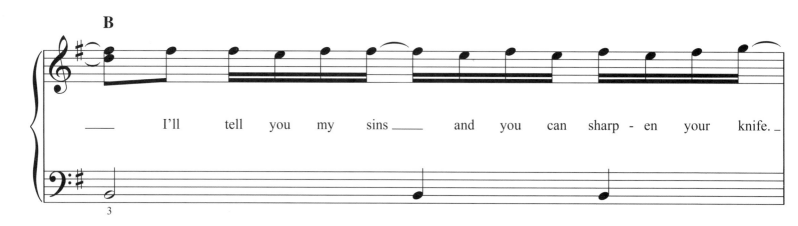